GO EXTREME!

BE A PRO SURFER

By Lynda Arnez

Gareth Stevens PUBLISHING

Please visit our website, www.garethstevens.com. For a free color catalog of all our high-quality books, call toll free 1-800-542-2595 or fax 1-877-542-2596.

Library of Congress Cataloging-in-Publication Data
Names: Arnéz, Lynda, author.
Title: Be a pro surfer / Lynda Arnez.
Description: Buffalo, New York : Gareth Stevens Publishing, [2024] | Series: Go extreme! | Includes index.
Identifiers: LCCN 2023009668 (print) | LCCN 2023009669 (ebook) | ISBN 9781538287026 (library binding) | ISBN 9781538287019 (paperback) | ISBN 9781538287033 (ebook)
Subjects: LCSH: Surfing–Juvenile literature. | Surfers–Juvenile literature. | Aquatic sports–Juvenile literature.
Classification: LCC GV840.S8 A76 2024 (print) | LCC GV840.S8 (ebook) | DDC 797.3/2–dc23/eng/20230301
LC record available at https://lccn.loc.gov/2023009668
LC ebook record available at https://lccn.loc.gov/2023009669

First Edition

Published in 2024 by
Gareth Stevens Publishing
2544 Clinton St
Buffalo, NY 14224

Designer: Ellen Weber
Editor: Kristen Rajczak Nelson

Photo credits: Cover, p. 1 Pressmaster/Shutterstock.com; pp. 5, 19 homydesign/Shutterstock.com; pp. 7, 17, 27 Mana Photo/Shutterstock.com; p. 9 manpeppe/Shutterstock.com; p. 11 LouisLotterPhotography/Shutterstock.com; p. 13 Elizaveta Galitckaia/Shutterstock.com; p. 15 Flystock/Shutterstock.com; pp. 21, 25 Denis Moskvinov/Shutterstock.com; p. 21 Joao Serafim/Shutterstock.com; p. 23 Anton Watman/Shutterstock.com; p. 29 jarvis gray/Shutterstock.com; p. 30 Volina/Shutterstock.com; Series Art Mind Pixell/Shutterstock.com; Series Art Duda Vasilii/Shutterstock.com; Series Art PegasuStudio/Shutterstock.com; Series Art Scott Webb/Pexels.com.

Printed in the United States of America

Some of the images in this book illustrate individuals who are models. The depictions do not imply actual situations or events.

CPSIA compliance information: Batch #CS24GS: For further information contact Gareth Stevens, New York, New York at 1-800-542-2595.

CONTENTS

THE G.O.A.T.

As a teen, surfing **legend** Kelly Slater won **competitions** around the world. He turned pro around age 18, and within a few years became the biggest name in surfing. His success is one-in-a-million! The path to becoming a pro surfer is hard work—and very competitive.

PUSHING THE LIMITS

As of 2022, Slater has been named world champion, or winner of his sport, 11 times! He is called the G.O.A.T of surfing, which stands for greatest of all time.

ALL ABOUT THE PROS

"Pro" is short for professional. This means that someone gets paid to do a job, including play or take part in a sport. In some sports, like surfing, pro may mean an **athlete** who competes at a high level.

PUSHING THE LIMITS

Pro surfer John John Florence was part of Team USA at the Olympics held in Tokyo, Japan, in 2021. It was the first time surfing was part of the Olympics.

John John Florence

The top pros in surfing compete in two **circuits**. Pros in the World **Qualifying** Series compete in events around the world to earn points. Those with the most points can become part of the highest circuit in competitive surfing: the Championship Tour (CT).

PUSHING THE LIMITS

There aren't many spots on the CT. There are fewer spots for women than men.

THE COST TO GO PRO

Surfing can be an expensive, or costly, sport. Surfers have to travel all over the world for the biggest competitions. Plus, surfers need the right surfboards for the different kinds of waves they are surfing, among other gear. All that adds up.

PUSHING THE LIMITS

Stephanie Gilmore began surfing professionally at age 17. She's an eight-time world champion!

Stephanie Gilmore

SURF SPONSORSHIP

Surfers become professional when they get their first sponsor. Sponsors are companies or **brands** that give surfers money or gear. In turn, surfers wear and use this gear to promote, or bring attention to, their sponsors. At first, sponsors may just send clothes or sunscreen!

PUSHING THE LIMITS

Winning **amateur** surf contests is one way to get noticed by sponsors.

As surfers have more success, their sponsorships get bigger. Sponsors may pay for pros to travel to the biggest surf competitions. They may give pros extra money for doing well or winning too. Sponsorships allow surfers to spend as much time surfing as they can.

PUSHING THE LIMITS

Surfers have often been thought to be laid back and easy-going. But pro surfers must work hard to get and keep sponsors!

Few pro surfers make the millions of dollars other sports stars do. Those who compete well make prize money, in addition to drawing in sponsors. But many need another job in order to have enough money to keep entering surfing competitions.

PUSHING THE LIMITS

Another way surfers can gain sponsors is through social media. Having a large following and cool personal style can get a brand's attention too.

Jamie O'Brien

Once a surfer makes it to the CT and has a big sponsor, they have it made, right? Even the pros on the CT have to work to keep their spot on it! That means pro surfers are always working to get better.

PUSHING THE LIMITS

Brazilian pro surfer Gabriel Medina is one of the top young surfers on the CT. He's known to be hard to beat!

Gabriel Medina

GETTING STARTED

Kids who want to be pro surfers can get started as soon as they're near the ocean! Many pro surfers were first taught to surf by family members. If no one in your family surfs, you can hire a surf instructor, or teacher.

PUSHING THE LIMITS

Thanks to a new kind of pool, people who don't live near the ocean may still be able to learn to surf. Pools that make waves are being built all over the world!

surf wave pool, Switzerland

SURF FITNESS

Surfers work hard to stay fit in and out of the water. First, you need to surf a lot! You'll learn to read the waves. You also need to work on holding your breath. And you must have a strong upper body.

PUSHING THE LIMITS

A big reason surfers travel around the world is to surf the best waves. They know what times of the year the waves will be best in a place!

READY TO COMPETE

Once you know the basics of surfing, you may want to enter a competition! At first, these help you learn. You can find out what you are good at and what you need to work on.

PUSHING THE LIMITS

The youngest surfers in a competition are often called "groms." This is short for grommet, which is the lowest group of people working on a ship in a navy.

TIME FOR STYLE

Once you compete a bit, it's time to work on your style. Great style while riding a wave can bring in sponsors even if you don't win yet! This may include learning tricks. No matter what you are doing, always follow safety rules when out surfing!

PUSHING THE LIMITS

Big wave surfers take on waves that may be 60 feet (18 m) tall! Keala Kennelly is known as one of the best surfers in big wave surfing today.

Keala Kennelly

It's a lot of work to become a pro surfer—and even more work to stay on top. But surfers can have long **careers**. Kelly Slater won a big competition called the Billabong Pro Pipeline in 2022 just before he turned 50!

PUSHING THE LIMITS

One thing all pros share is a love for the ocean and surfing! Even when it's hard work, remember to enjoy surfing, and you'll feel like a pro.

Kelly Slater at Billabong Pro Pipeline

SURF'S UP!

These are some of the best places in the world to surf!

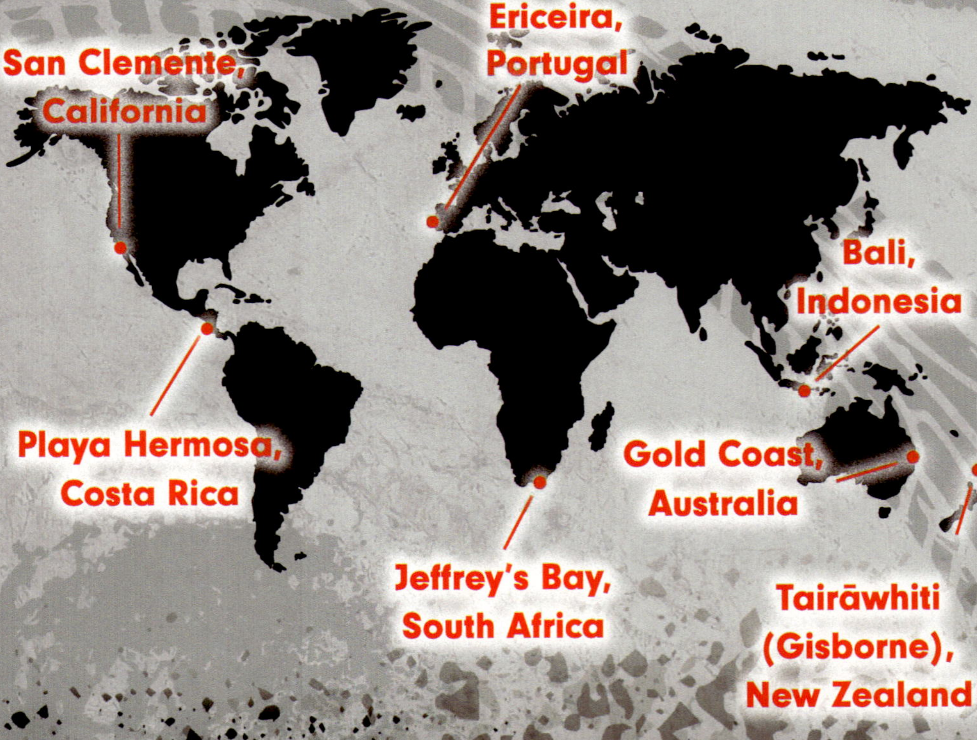

FOR MORE INFORMATION

BOOKS

Carr, Aaron. *Surfing*. New York, NY: AV2, 2021.

Lyon, Drew. *Big-Time Extreme Sports Records*. North Mankato, MN: Capstone Press, 2022.

WEBSITES

Surf Etiquette for Beginners

tommytsunamisurfschool.com/how-to-learn-surfing-blog/surf-etiquette-for-beginners-12-things-every-beginner-surfer-should-know/

Read about safety and being a good surfing citizen on this website, as well as get tips for learning to surf.

USA Surfing

www.usasurfing.org/

Keep up with the best U.S. surfers on the home site of USA Surfing.

Publisher's note to educators and parents: Our editors have carefully reviewed these websites to ensure that they are suitable for students. Many websites change frequently, however, and we cannot guarantee that a site's future contents will continue to meet our high standards of quality and educational value. Be advised that students should be closely supervised whenever they access the internet.

GLOSSARY

amateur: Having to do with someone who does not get paid to take part in a sport or hobby.

athlete: Someone who takes part in a sport.

brand: A group of products made by a company under a certain name.

career: A job one does for a long time.

circuit: A series of sports events held in different places.

competition: A contest someone tries to win against others. Competitive means having to do with people trying to win a competition or become more successful than others.

legend: A person in a sport who is known for their skill and winning record.

qualify: To win the right to be a part of something.

INDEX